ALBUM ARTWORK: © 1998 MAVERICK/
WARNER BROS. RECORDS

PROJECT MANAGER: JEANNETTE DELISA
ART LAYOUT: MARCELA PEREZ

© 1998 WARNER BROS. PUBLICATIONS
ALL RIGHTS RESERVED

WARNER BROS. PUBLICATIONS - THE GLOBAL LEADER IN PRINT
USA: 15800 NW 48th Avenue, Miami, FL 33014

WARNER/CHAPPELL MUSIC
CANADA: 85 SCARSDALE ROAD, SUITE 101
DON MILLS, ONTARIO, M3B 2R2
SCANDINAVIA: P.O. BOX 533, VENDEVAGEN 85 B
S-182 15, DANDERYD, SWEDEN
AUSTRALIA: P.O. BOX 353
3 TALAVERA ROAD, NORTH RYDE N.S.W. 2113

NUOVA CARISCH
ITALY: VIA CAMPANIA, 12
20098 S. GIULIANO MILANESE (MI)
ZONA INDUSTRIALE SESTO ULTERIANO
SPAIN: MAGALLANES, 25
28015 MADRID
FRANCE: 25 RUE DE HAUTEVILLE, 75010 PARIS

IMP
INTERNATIONAL MUSIC PUBLICATIONS LIMITED
ENGLAND: SOUTHEND ROAD,
WOODFORD GREEN, ESSEX IG8 8HN
GERMANY: MARSTALLSTR. 8, D-80539 MUNCHEN
DENMARK: DANMUSIK, VOGNMAGERGADE 7
DK 1120 KOBENHAVNK

CW00945803

13.99

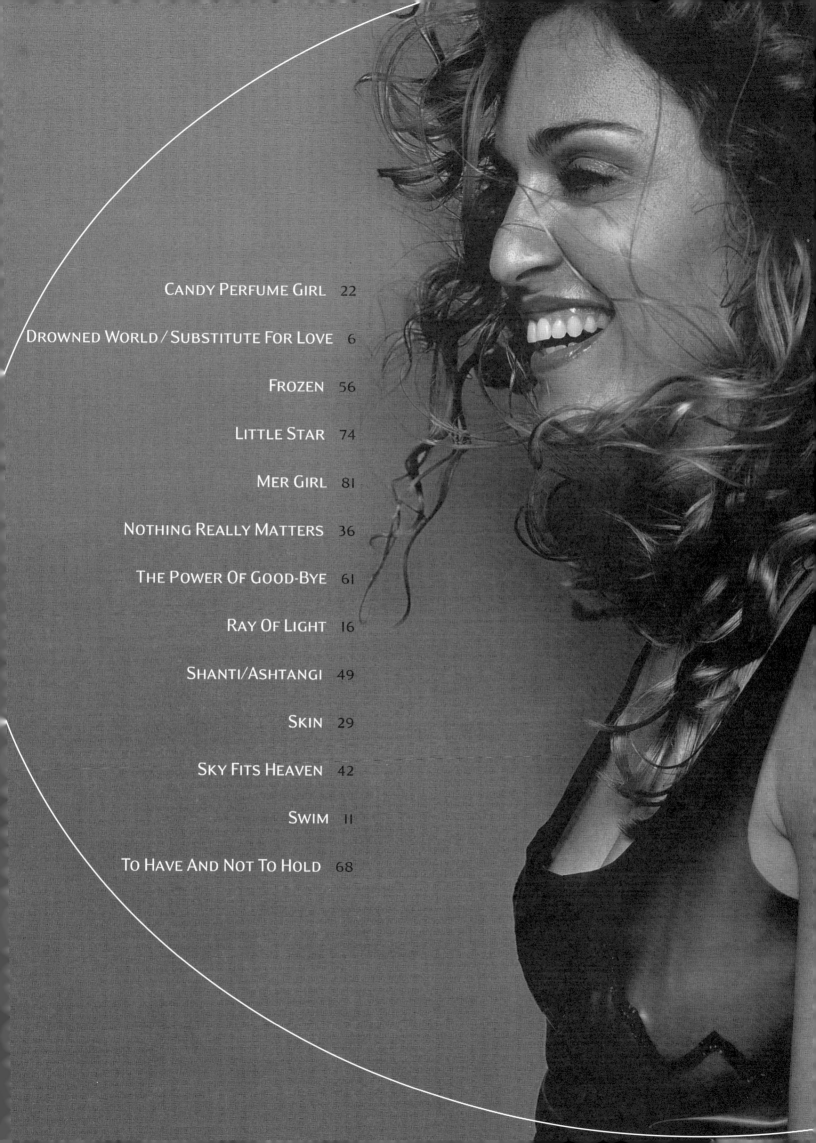

DROWNED WORLD/
SUBSTITUTE FOR LOVE

Words and Music by
MADONNA CICCONE, DAVID COLLINS,
WILLIAM ORBIT, ROD MCKUEN and ANITA KERR

Drowned World/Substitute for Love - 5 - 1
0263B

8

feel-ing so a-lone. I had so man-y lov-ers who set-tled for the thrill_ of

bask-ing in my spot-light. I nev-er felt so hap - py.

Mm, mm_____ mm._____

Chorus:

The face of you, my sub-sti-tute_ for_ love, my sub-sti-tute_ for_ love. Mm._____

Should I wait_ for you, my sub-sti-tute_ for_ love, my sub-sti-tute_ for_ love?

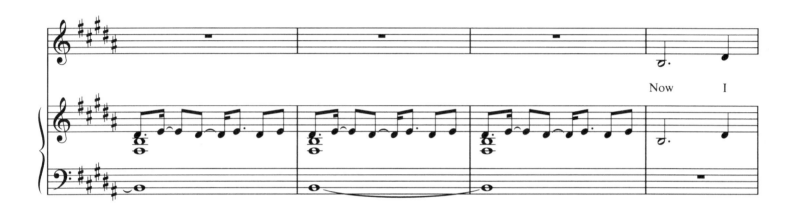

Now I

N.C.

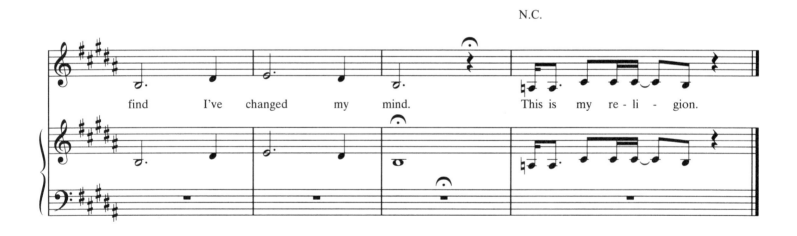

find I've changed my mind. This is my re - li - gion.

Verse 3:
Famous faces, far-off places, trinkets I can buy,
No handsome stranger, petty danger job that I can try.
No ferris wheel, no heart to steal, no laughter in the dark,
No one-night stand, no far-off land, no fire that I can spark.
(To Chorus:)

SWIM

Words and Music by
MADONNA CICCONE
and WILLIAM ORBIT

14

RAY OF LIGHT

Words and Music by
MADONNA CICCONE, WILLIAM ORBIT,
CHRISTINE LEACH, CLIVE MULDOON and DAVE CURTIS

1. Zeph-yr in the sky__ at night,__ I won-der__ do my tears__ of
2. Fast-er than the speed-ing light,__ she's fly-ing,__ try-ing to__ re-

mourn-ing__ sink be-neath the sun?_____
mem-ber__ where it all__ be-gan.

21

Ray of Light - 6 - 6
0263B

CANDY PERFUME GIRL

Words and Music by
MADONNA CICCONE,
WILLIAM ORBIT and SUSANNAH MELVOIN

23

SKIN

Words and Music by
MADONNA CICCONE and
PATRICK LEONARD

skin._____ I

soul._____ I've

close my eyes.___ I need to make__ a con - nec -

got this thing.___ I want to make__ a cor - rec -

tion. I'm walk - ing on___ a thin

tion. I'm not like this___ all the

line._____

time._____ You've got this thing.___

I close my eyes.___

NOTHING REALLY MATTERS

Words and Music by
MADONNA CICCONE and
PATRICK LEONARD

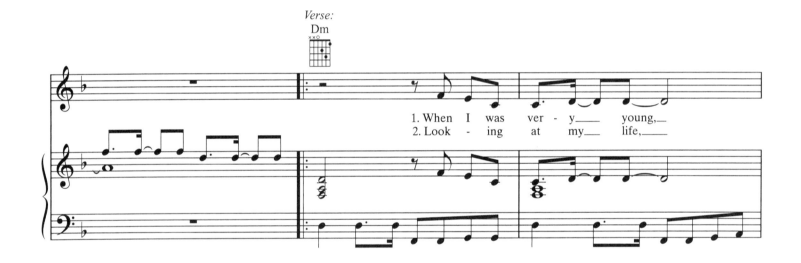

1. When I was ver - y___ young,___
2. Look - ing at my___ life,___

noth-ing real - ly mat - tered___ to me___ but mak - ing___ my
it's ver - y clear to___ me.___ I lived___ so

SKY FITS HEAVEN

Words and Music by
MADONNA CICCONE and
PATRICK LEONARD

44

46

Bridge:

Trav - el - ing down___ my own road,

watch - ing the signs___ as I

go.___

Trav - el - ing down___ my own road,___

Sky Fits Heaven - 7 - 5
0263B

SHANTI/ASHTANGI

Words and Music by
MADONNA CICCONE and
WILLIAM ORBIT

50

52

shan - ti, shan - ti, shan - ti____ ohm.____

Repeat ad lib. and fade

(Instrumental)

FROZEN

Words and Music by
MADONNA CICCONE and
PATRICK LEONARD

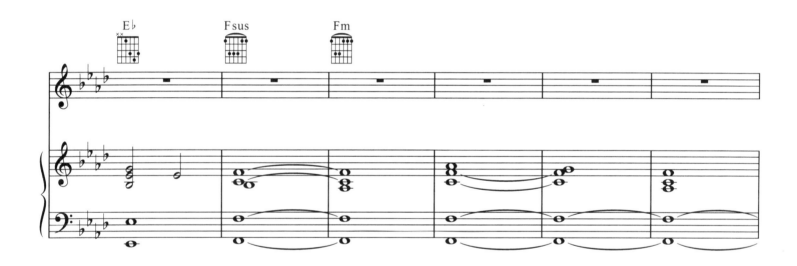

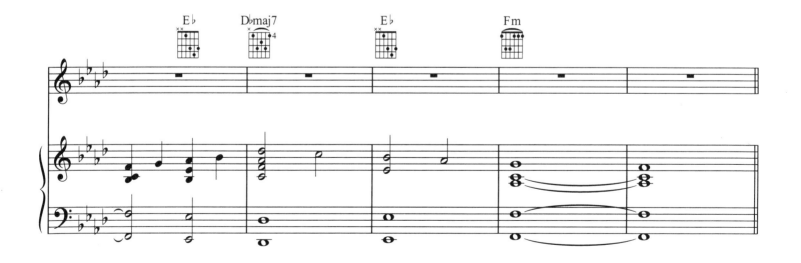

58

Frozen - 5 - 3
0263B

the key.   If I could melt your___ heart.

THE POWER OF GOOD-BYE

Words and Music by
MADONNA CICCONE
and RICK NOWELS

The Power of Good-Bye - 7 - 1
0263B

62

2. You were my

Verses 2 & 3:

les - son   I had to learn.   I was your

3. *See additional lyrics*
4. *Instrumental solo ad lib....*

for - tress   you had to burn.

Pain is a warn - ing that some-thing's wrong. I pray to God__ that it won't be long.

64

The Power of Good-Bye - 7 - 5
0263B

66

The Power of Good-Bye - 7 - 6
0263B

Verse 3:
Your heart is not open, so I must go.
The spell has been broken, I loved you so.
You were my lesson I had to learn,
I was your fortress.

Chorus 2:
There's nothing left to lose.
There's no more heart to bruise.
There's no greater power than the power of good-bye.

TO HAVE AND NOT TO HOLD

Words and Music by
MADONNA CICCONE
and RICK NOWELS

LITTLE STAR

Words and Music by
MADONNA CICCONE
and RICK NOWELS

Fast, with 2 feel ♩ = 140

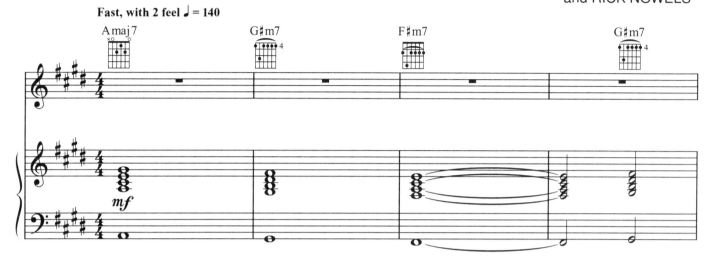

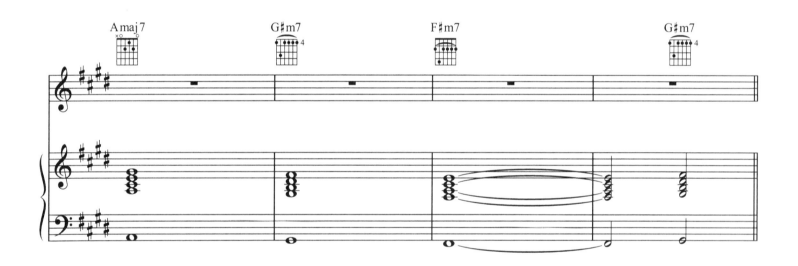

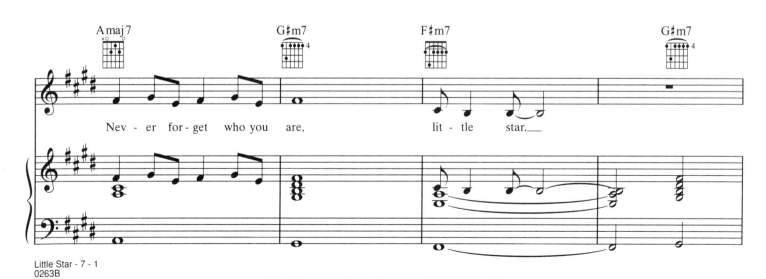

Nev - er for - get who you are, lit - tle star.___

MER GIRL

Words and Music by
MADONNA CICCONE
and WILLIAM ORBIT

Slowly ♩. = 72

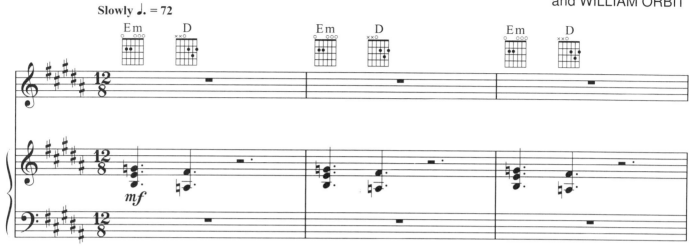

1. I ran from my house that can-not con-tain me,

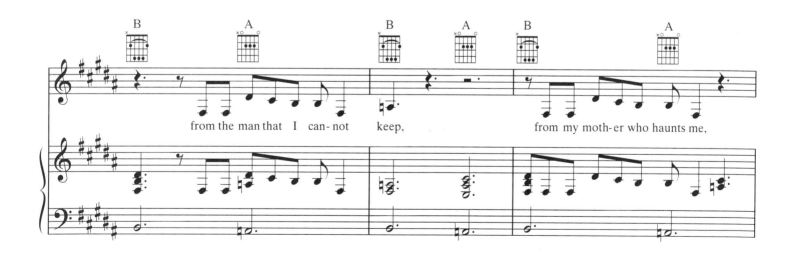

from the man that I can-not keep, from my moth-er who haunts me,

Mer Girl - 7 - 1
0263B

83

Mer Girl - 7 - 3
0263B